A SMART CHOICE TO MAKE

ISBN: 978-3-9525007-4-3

ABOUT THE AUTHOR:

Mara Catherine Harvey

I am passionately driven by two strong beliefs: that we cannot wait another 100+ years to see economic gender equality come to life, and that daily financial decisions are the most untapped source of positive social change. These convictions are at the heart of my stories.

Over the past two decades, my work in the financial industry led me to explore the profound differences in the ways men and women approach wealth. Very often women feel less financially confident than men in managing money. Research shows that money messages are biased and this bias starts at a very young age. So I decided to find a playful way to convey important money messages around equality, earning, saving, spending and sustainability to young children, and to girls in particular. Because money is not just a transmission of value: it's a transmission of values.

Book 1: A Smart Way to Start
Book 2: A Smart Way to Save
Book 3: A Smart Way to Spend
Book 4: A Smart Choice to Make

For more information: www.smartwaytostart.com

ABOUT THE ILLUSTRATOR:

Mariajosé Gajate Molina

(MARIAJO ILUSTRAJO)

Loving drawing since I can remember, I followed my passion studying illustration at the art school *Arte10*, in Madrid. I've been a freelance illustrator since then, completing projects for a wide range of clients.

Learning never stops, so some years later I moved to Bath where I studied Graphic Communication at Bath Spa University.

I enjoy learning new ways of working, developing new styles or just getting my hands dirty. Nothing is more important than loving what you do ("sketcher, traveller and tea drinker"). I always carry a pencil and a notebook in my bag. Maybe you´ll find me doodling in a cafe!

Currently I am studying MA Childrens Book Illustration at Anglia Ruskin in Cambridge to continue improving and having fun.

If you want to know a bit more about me:
www.mariajoilustrajo.com

DEDICATED TO ALL THE CHILDREN WHO ARE GOING TO MAKE THIS WORLD A BETTER PLACE! AND TO ALL THE PEOPLE WHO SUPPORT THEM IN MAKING WISE CHOICES!

You earned lots of pennies and saved quite a few.
You're planning to go out and buy something new.
Did you know that your money can impact this world
in a positive way? Why, haven't you heard?

How curious are you? Do you want to see
how much better this world could certainly be?
When you spend your money, what does it do?
Do you choose wisely, whom you give it to?

So let me explain just how great you can be!
Your choices will matter immensely, you'll see!

When you buy something, your pennies will go
to a firm which then uses your money to grow.
With all of your money, firms make things galore,
and the question is *how*? Do you want to know more?

PAPER
FACTORY

T-SHIRT FACTORY

PLASTIC
FACTORY

Let's look at nature, a good place to start.
To protect it we really have got to be smart!
Yet some firms do damage, like cutting down trees.
Some firms throw rubbish or plastic in seas.
If you had your say, would you let them destroy?
Shouldn't nature be something we all can *enjoy*?

Why does it matter? Well let's stop and think.
Pollution is growing and some rivers stink!
Fish cannot live, and the sea can't survive.
As food becomes scarcer, no animals thrive.
It really is dreadful, but now you must know
your spending can change this, so simply say: "No!"
Don't buy from a firm if it does too much harm
Don't give them your money:
say no and keep calm!

PAPER FACTORY
WASTE WATER FROM FACTORY

Yes, each penny matters, and you have a choice.
By spending your money, you're using your voice.
This is the good news, it's all up to you!
You can decide what your pennies should do.

If you make good choices, you can save the earth!
And this is what makes your money's true worth!
So when you spend money, choose brands that do well,
that take care of nature, and openly tell
how products are made, and impact our land,
our animals, plants and the air all around.

MONEY FOR THINGS
THAT ARE GOOD
FOR THE PLANET

Another dimension, you must be aware,
is how firms treat workers and whether they care.
Do they make sure that children aren't slaves
and forced to work very very long days?

For this is a shameful and terrible plight,
it really needs people who stand up and fight!
People who say "I won't put money there!
I won't buy from firms that don't seem to care".

Children should never be forced to miss school,
they need education and this is a rule!
Even on days when school isn't fun,
it's better to learn, and once they've begun,
it gives them a chance to decide what they'll be:
any or all of the things that they dream!

6 x 7 = 42
6 x 8 = 48
6 x 9 = 54
6 x 10 = 60

So make your voice heard, by asking to know,
to which kind of firms your pennies will go.
Just ask and you'll see that the answers will come.
Your journey to make this world good has begun!

Do firms care for oceans,
for dolphins and fish?
And care how the food's made,
that lands on your dish?
Do they use cleaner energy
for what they do?
Do they care for the water,
and saving it, too?

Do they try to find ways
to be kind to the earth?
And avoid just producing
to maximize worth?
Do they reduce waste,
and limit their use
of poisons, of plastics,
of other refuse?

Do they care for the trees
and the plants and the flowers?
Do they care that their people
don't work too long hours?
Do they try to find ways
for resources to last?
Do they try not to make
the mistakes of the past?

This might sound quite easy, but sometimes it's not.
In haste to make money, some people forgot
that you simply can't use up resources so fast
without hurting our planet, we need it to last!

Take fashion, we all like to buy fancy clothes.
But we've taken this business as far as it goes...
Did you know that clothing is one of the worst
biggest polluters across all our earth?

FACT

= 2.700 LITRES

OF WATER

(ALMOST 20 BATHTUBS)

On the list of bad impact, right up there with oil!
Who would have known there's so much it would spoil!

Each day when you choose what you're going to wear,
think about: How was this made? And where?
Was it made being mindful that colours need dye,
and that waste in the water makes poor fishes die?
Was it made without forcing small children to work,
making sure they're at school and can do their homework?

We all must find ways to not waste and not hurt.
It's a choice that we make every day with our purse!

It's true that *good* things might cost a bit more.
But the true cost of "cheap" is often way more!
It just isn't us who carry that cost.
It's others, in countries where nature is lost.

So when you go shopping, please be well aware,
that you can choose brands which really do care!

Whatever it is that your pennies are for,
You have a real chance to demand so much more:
Whether you want cleaner oceans and seas,
Whether you'll save all the birds and the bees,
Whether you want cleaner energy too,
Whether your lifestyle is healthy for you.

You might still be young, but you have a voice!
You just need to know this, and make it your choice.
Whenever you spend, beware of your power!
You're changing this world - hour after hour!

SAVE THE
OCEANS!

So isn't it great?
Now *you* can do good!
It can be so simple, if it's understood.
Ask for those things that do matter to you.
And choose your brands wisely,
it's easy to do!

Now that you know
there is a *good* way,
Be happy and think:
today is *my* day!
Today I can choose,
today I can start!
When I buy, when I spend,
I can be super smart!

You've come to the last line of book number four,
And yes, you guessed right: there is more to explore!
Join us online and meet Marty & friends,
Her story goes on and this isn't the end...

WWW.SMARTWAYTOSTART.COM/MARTY

Printed in Great Britain
by Amazon

11868411R00018